THE THEATRE OF ILLUSION

Other Works by Richard Wilbur

The Beautiful Changes and Other Poems
Ceremony and Other Poems
A Bestiary (editor, with Alexander Calder)
Molière's *The Misanthrope* (translator)
Things of this World
Poems 1943–1956
Candide: A Comic Operetta Based on Voltaire's Satire
(with Lillian Hellman)
Poe: Complete Poems (editor)
Advice to a Prophet and Other Poems
Molière's *Tartuffe* (translator)
The Poems of Richard Wilbur
Loudmouse (for children)
Shakespeare: Poems (coeditor, with Alfred Harbage)
Walking to Sleep: New Poems and Translations
Molière's *The School for Wives* (translator)
Opposites
The Mind-Reader: New Poems
Responses: Prose Pieces, 1948–1976
Molière's *The Learned Ladies* (translator)
The Whale and Other Uncollected Translations
Molière's *Four Comedies* (translator)
Racine's *The Andromache* (translator)
Racine's *Phaedra* (translator)
New and Collected Poems
Molière's *The School for Husbands* (translator)
More Opposites
Molière's *Imaginary Cuckold, or Sganarelle* (translator)
Molière's *Amphitryon* (translator)
Runaway Opposites (for children)
The Catbird's Song: Prose Pieces, 1963–1995
Molière's *Don Juan* (translator)
The Disappearing Alphabet (for children)
Mayflies: New Poems and Translations
The Pig in the Spigot (for children)
Poe: Poems and Poetics (editor)
Collected Poems 1943–2004

Pierre Corneille

The
'Theatre
of Illusion

———————

Translated and with an Introduction by
Richard Wilbur

A Harvest Original • Harcourt, Inc.

Orlando   Austin   New York   San Diego   Toronto   London

Act Two, Scene Two, of this translation appeared in *Poetry.*
Scenes Three through Six in Act Two appeared in the *Yale Review.*

www.HarcourtBooks.com

Library of Congress Cataloging-in-Publication-Data
Corneille, Pierre, 1606–1684.
[Illusion comique. English]
The theatre of illusion/by Pierre Corneille; translated and with
an introduction by Richard Wilbur.
p. cm.—(A Harvest book)
I. Wilbur, Richard, 1921– II. Title.
PQ1755.I5E5 2007
842'.4—dc22 2006034864
ISBN 978-0-15-603231-5

Text set in Adobe Garamond
Designed by Cathy Riggs

Printed in the United States of America
First edition
A C E G I K J H F D B

For Bill and Sonja

INTRODUCTION

Pierre Corneille, in dedicating this play to a mysterious Mademoiselle M.F.D.R., described it as a "strange monster," and went on to say, "The first act is a mere prologue, the next three acts are an unfinished comedy, the last is a tragedy: and all this, stitched together, adds up to a comedy." *The Theatre of Illusion* (1636), which Corneille elsewhere described as a "caprice" and an "extravagant trifle," is almost the only work of its kind in his large oeuvre; in its own moment it pleased its audiences, but it vanished from the stage during the prevalence of classical standards. In 1937 the great actor Louis Jouvet revived the play at the Comédie Française, with sets and costumes by Christian Bérard, and it has since been widely judged to be, in Virginia Scott's words, "Corneille's baroque masterpiece."

It might be argued that the play represents Pridamant's quest for his alienated son Clindor—a quest that is resolved in one day by means of visions summoned up in Alcandre's magic cave. Thus described, the play could seem to possess the three unities of time, place, and action on which the French Academy—founded by Richelieu in 1635—was to insist. However, the central story of Clindor and Isabelle, which is but framed by the brief colloquies of Pridamant and Alcandre, does not at all comply with the classical formula. There is a four-day interval toward the end of act 3, a two-year lapse before act 4 begins. The location changes with Shakespearean license between various levels of a Bordeaux mansion, a prison cell, a Parisian stage-set representing an English garden. And what about unity of theme and action? Suffice it to say that the most delightful character in the play, the boastful and craven Matamore, is not really essential to the plot, performs in a farcical key of his own, and was invented—as Corneille acknowledged in his *Examen* of 1660—"purely for laughter's sake."

The Theatre of Illusion is in every way exhilaratingly free of formula. To speak further of its characters, the handsome young hero Clindor is consistently witty and articulate, but has the fundamental elusiveness of the picaresque rascal. We do not know what he will do, say, or pretend to be; he is, one might say, an actor. The moment of true heroism in the play—the moment of Cornelian self-conquest—is surprisingly allotted in act 4, scene 3, to the servant girl Lyse, and Corneille confessed that at times Lyse is nobler and loftier than convention would lead one to expect. The modes of comedy, tragedy, and farce are intermingled so that none imposes a predictable machinery, and the audience enjoys not one pattern of art but a fluent, runaway artifice. There are many scenes of deception-followed-by-enlightenment: Lyse's callous teasing of Isabelle at the beginning of act 4, scene 2, the jailer's hoaxing of Clindor in act 4, scene 8, Alcandre's toying with Pridamant's despair in act 5, scene 5. There are other times as well in which Pridamant, watching the illusions conjured up by Alcandre, forgets the latter's sanguine reassurances; in these alarms and incertitudes, the actual audience of the play will sometimes join him.

Nowhere is this more the case than in act 5. There the audience, and their proxy Pridamant, behold a vision of the principals in action, and that play-within-a-play is in its turn the conclusion of a tragic drama in which Isabelle, Clindor, and Lyse are at the moment performing. The density of illusion is further deepened by the fact that, though Clindor and Isabelle are playing the roles of "Théagène" and "Hippolyte," those names are never uttered in the dialogue, and the qualities of those characters are reminiscent of their own: Théagène and Hippolyte have fled her father's house together; Théagène, like Clindor, is a philanderer; Hippolyte, like Isabelle, speaks of rejoining her beloved in death. The murder of Théagène is accomplished by a character—Éraste—whose name is never spoken, but whose incursion seems a reprise of Adraste's in act 3. In the house of mirrors which is act 5, Corneille portrays the professional success of the main characters, and at the same time so identifies Clindor with Théagène as to "deceive Clindor's father . . . by a seeming death, and render his recovery from grief to joy more surprising and pleasing." So said Corneille, looking back on the play in 1660.

The play ends as a celebration of the theatre, but it also belongs to an era in which theatre was a metaphor for the illusory nature of human life. Shakespeare's Prospero had summoned up actor-spirits to entertain Miranda and Ferdinand, and in dismissing them had said that we, like them, "are such stuff / As dreams are made on." The baroque church of S. Ignazio in Rome, famous for its trompe l'oeil ceiling frescoes by Andrea dal Pozzo, faced upon a square suggestive of a theatre, and the departing worshipper might see himself as leaving the realities of the altar for the vain shows of the world. With all its ambiguity, surprise, and magic, *L'Illusion comique* plays charmingly with such a sense of things.

My English version has preserved the rhymed couplets of the original, and has aimed at a thought-for-thought fidelity to the text; I trust also to have been faithful in regard to tone, which is the crucial thing in all translation. Here and there, in hopes that my lines will be acted or read aloud, I have used stress marks to show where the emphasis should go. I have imagined the characters' names as pronounced in a manner roughly French, but without strain; in the case of Lyse, my preference is for LEE-za.

I thank my friend Franklin Reeve for urging me to do this translation, and my wife, as always, for advising me at every step.

R. W.
Cummington, 2006

CHARACTERS

ALCANDRE, a magician
PRIDAMANT, Clindor's father
DORANTE, a friend of Pridamant's
MATAMORE, a Gascon soldier, suitor of Isabelle
CLINDOR, aide to Matamore, lover of Isabelle
ADRASTE, a gentleman, suitor of Isabelle
GÉRONTE, father of Isabelle
ISABELLE, daughter of Géronte
LYSE (pronounced LISA), Isabelle's maid
A JAILER
PAGE hired by Matamore
CLINDOR in the role of THÉAGÈNE, an English lord
ISABELLE in the role of HIPPOLYTE, Théagène's wife
LYSE in the role of CLARINE, Hippolyte's maid-in-waiting
ÉRASTE, equerry of Théagène's patron Florilame
A Troop of ADRASTE'S SERVANTS
A Troop of FLORILAME'S SERVANTS

*The scene is in Touraine, in the countryside near
the Magician's cave*

ACT I

Scene I

PRIDAMANT, DORANTE

DORANTE

This wizard, though all nature is his slave,
Has made his palace in that gloomy cave.
In those dread premises, a perpetual night
Yields only to a strange, unearthly light
Which, with its ghostly luminescence, aids
The summoning of spirits and of shades.
Stand back; his art has charmed these boulders here
To punish anyone who comes too near,
And in that cave-mouth the enchanted air
Has hardened to a wall, and serves him there
As an unseen rampart able to oppose
And scatter in the dust a thousand foes.
But privacy concerns him most; he sees
Intruders as far worse than enemies;
And so, however eager, you must bide
Your time till he's no longer occupied.
Each day he takes the air, and I've no doubt
That very soon he will be coming out.

PRIDAMANT

I long to see him, yet my doubts remain.
I'm eager, yet I fear my hopes are vain.

The son for whom I feel such dear concern,
Who grew estranged because I was too stern,
And whom I've sought for ten years, high and low,
Is now forever lost to me, I know.
Thinking him willful and a little wild,
I laid strict disciplines upon my child,
Meaning to tame his spirit; but, sad to say,
My strictness only made him run away.
I saw that I had blindly overstepped;
I'd raged at him, but when he fled, I wept,
And my paternal love soon bred in me
Just guilt for my unjust severity.
I sought him, seeing in my travels then
The Po, the Rhine, the Tagus, and the Seine,
But there was no abatement of my grief;
My useless wanderings brought me no relief.
At length, despairing of such labor lost
And doubtful that I could at any cost
Contrive by human wit to end my woe,
I turned for counsel to the powers below.
I met the great practitioners of that science
On which Alcandre places his reliance.
They all were highly praised, as he by you,
But for my sorrows nothing could they do.
To me, the spirit world has naught to say,
Or says it only in a riddling way.

DORANTE

Alcandre is no ordinary man.
He does things that no other wizard can.

4

I shall not tell you how he wields the thunder,
Troubles the ocean, cracks the earth asunder,
Whips up a thousand hurricanes, and throws
Battalions of the same against his foes,
How with a mystic word or two he forces
Mountains to move and clouds to change their courses,
Or bids the sun shine at the midnight hour.
But you've no need of such displays of power:
Enough that he can read men's minds, and sees
The future and the past with equal ease.
To know all secrets he has but to look:
For him, our destinies are an open book.
Like you, I once was skeptical. Yet when we
First met, he told me all my history,
And I was staggered, hearing him lay bare
The details of my every love affair.

PRIDAMANT

You tell great things of him.

DORANTE

                    And could tell more.

PRIDAMANT

In vain you seek to raise my spirits, for
I know I'll still be in this mournful plight
When my sad days must end in endless night.

DORANTE

Since I left Brittany with the desire
Of coming here to be a country squire,
And in a two years' courtship prospered so
That I've a wife now and a fine chateau,
All who've consulted him have been content;
I don't know one who thought the time misspent.
Trust me: his help is nothing you should spurn.
Besides, he loves to do me a good turn,
And I dare boast that if I make a few
Entreaties, he'll do wondrous things for you.

PRIDAMANT

That fate could be so kind, I still must doubt.

DORANTE

Cheer up, my friend; the sage is coming out,
And walks to meet us. His all-knowing soul,
Which holds all nature under its control,
Could not preserve from time, these hundred years,
More than the skeleton he now appears;
And yet his bodily strength does not abate,
His limbs are supple and his bearing straight:
Mysterious forces drive this old man's heart,
And all his steps are miracles of art.

Scene II

DORANTE

Great learnèd spirit, you whose studious nights
Produce each day new wonders and delights,
You to whom all our plans are known, and who,
Not seeing us, can yet see all we do,
If ever by your art's great potency
You have seen fit to be of aid to me,
Then heal this father's deep unhappiness.
As an old friend, I feel for his distress.
Like me, he comes from Rennes. In my young days
He showed me kindness in a hundred ways,
And there his son, in age and rank my peer,
Became a friend both intimate and dear . . .

ALCANDRE

Enough, Dorante. What brings him here, I know.
That son's the reason for his present woe.
Old man, was not his leaving home the source
Of your incessant pain and just remorse?
Did not a stubborn strictness on your part
Drive him away from you, and break your heart?
And do you not, repenting what you've done,
Search everywhere for your maltreated son?

7

PRIDAMANT

O modern oracle, to whom all is plain,
I could not hide from you my guilt and pain.
You know my unjust rigor all too well,
The secrets of my heart you clearly tell.
It's true, I've erred; but surely for that wrong
My fruitless penance has been hard and long.
Pray set some limit to my anguished tears;
Give back the prop of my declining years.
If you have news of him, my heart will bound,
And love will lend me wings till he is found.
Where is he hiding? Pray you tell me where:
Were it the world's end, I would hasten there.

ALCANDRE

Take heart, old man. My magic shall provide you
With what the vengeful heavens have denied you.
You'll see your son again, crowned with success;
He's turned his banishment to happiness.
But words are nothing: to please Dorante and you,
I'll put the splendor of his lot on view.
Novice magicians, with their incense and
Their mumbled words that none can understand,
Their herbs, their perfumes, and their ritual,
Manage to make our art seem slow and dull;
But that's mere mumbo-jumbo, after all,
Intended to astonish or appall.
One gesture of my wand, and they're outdone.

(*He waves his wand and a curtain is drawn, behind
which the most beautiful costumes of an acting
troupe are displayed.*)
What does that wardrobe tell you of your son?
Come, Sir: could any prince be better dressed?
Can you see this, and fail to be impressed?

PRIDAMANT

Alas, you cater to a father's love;
Such rich attire my son's not worthy of;
It would be wrong for someone of his station
To walk abroad with so much ostentation.

ALCANDRE

Now that his fortunes have improved, and he
Has changed his rank in life accordingly,
No one could ever be offended by
His dressing thus when in the public eye.

PRIDAMANT

That pleasant thought I'll study to believe.
Some of those clothes are dresses, I perceive.
Is my son married?

ALCANDRE

      I gladly could recall
His loves and trials, and tell you of them all.
However, if the shock were not too great,

You could in an illusion contemplate
His life's adventures, played before your eyes
By spirits who put on a mortal guise
And have the power to speak and act, like us.

PRIDAMANT

You mustn't think that I am timorous.
How should I fear the image of a face
Which I have sought so long in many a place?

ALCANDRE (*To Dorante.*)

Pray leave us, Sir, and let this history be
A secret matter between him and me.

PRIDAMANT

I have no secrets from a friend so true.

DORANTE

What he commands, friend, we had better do.
I'll wait for you at home.

ALCANDRE

If he sees fit,
He'll give you, later, an account of it.

Scene III

ALCANDRE

Your son did not at once achieve high rank;
Not all his deeds were noble, to be frank,
And I'd be sorry, Sir, to itemize
His faults for any but his father's eyes.
He took some money from you as he went,
But by the second day that purse was spent;
To pay his way to Paris, he did the chore
Of selling headache powders door to door,
And told some fortunes, and so reached the town,
Where one must prosper by one's wits, or drown.
As a public scrivener he first found work,
Then, moving up, became a lawyer's clerk.
Bored by the pen, he next displayed a pair
Of dancing monkeys at a local fair.
He took to rhyming, writing many a ditty
Sung by the crude street-singers of the city,
And then developed a more polished style
In which he wrote romances for a while,
Jokes for Guillaume, and songs for Gautier.
Later, he dealt in amulets of bay
And all the nostrums of a master quack,

Until the law profession called him back.
In short, not even Lazarillo made
So many tricky shifts from trade to trade.
It's not a tale you'd like Dorante to hear.

PRIDAMANT

I'm grateful that you kept it from his ear.

ALCANDRE

My story's almost over, but I shall aim
To finish quickly and so spare you shame.
Weary of occupations vain and low,
He went, through some good fortune, to Bordeaux,
And there was hired to be the servant of
A local bravo who was daft with love.
That warrior engaged your son to be
His go-between, at a handsome salary.
He speaks his master's messages with style,
Shaking him down for money all the while,
And is in fact his master's rival, for
The lady clearly likes your son much more.
Once you have witnessed all their amorous story,
You'll see your son in all his pride and glory,
And what he's doing on this very day.

PRIDAMANT

Already, I feel my sorrow lift away.

ALCANDRE

In line with his profession, he became
Sir Clindor of the Mount, and by that name
You very soon may hear your son addressed.
Watch quietly, and in no way be distressed.
Your eagerness is such that my delay
Must aggravate you; but be patient, pray.
The speaking spirits whom you'll soon behold
Cannot by common magic be controlled.
Let's go into my cave, where I'll invent
New spells for this most rare experiment.

ACT II

Scene I

ALCANDRE

Don't be afraid, whatever you may see,
And do not leave this cave ahead of me,
On pain of death. Behold two phantoms who
Portray your dear son and his master, too.

PRIDAMANT

Oh, how my heart is straining to be near him!

ALCANDRE

Be silent. He's about to speak. Let's hear him.
(*Alcandre and Pridamant retire to one side of the stage.*)

Scene II

CLINDOR

Sir, why so restless? Is there any need,
With all your fame, for one more glorious deed?
Have you not slain enough bold foes by now,
And must you have fresh laurels for your brow?

MATAMORE

It's true, I'm restless, and I can't decide
Which of two foes should first be nullified—
The Mogul emperor or the Persian Sophy.

CLINDOR

Ah, let them live a while, Sir. Neither trophy
Would add a great deal to your fame and standing.
And where's the army that you'd be commanding?

MATAMORE

Army? Ah, villain, coward, do you doubt
That with this arm alone I'd wipe them out?
The mere sound of my name makes ramparts yield,
And drives divisions from the battlefield;

My wrath against these rulers needs engage
Only a piddling portion of my rage;
With one commandment given to the Fates
I oust the strongest monarchs from their states;
Thunder's my cannon; my troops, the Destinies;
One blow lays low a thousand enemies;
One breath, and all their hopes go up in smoke.
Yet you dare speak of armies! What a joke!
No longer shall a second Mars employ you;
With but a glance, you rogue, I shall destroy you . . .
And yet the thought of her whom I adore
Softens me now, and I'm enraged no more;
That little archer, whom every god obeys,
Forbids my eyes to glare with lethal rays.
Observe how my ferocity, which hates
And hacks and slaughters, gently dissipates
When I recall my lady, and my face
Is changed by thoughts of beauty, love, and grace.

CLINDOR

Oh, Sir, you have a hundred selves or more;
You're as handsome now as you were grim before.
I can't imagine any lady who
Could stubbornly refuse her heart to you.

MATAMORE

Whatever I may have said, feel no alarm:
Sometimes I terrify, sometimes I charm;
Depending on my humor, I inspire

Men with anxiety, women with desire.
Before I had the power to suppress
My beauty, women gave me much distress:
When I appeared, they swooned in quantity,
And thousands died each day for love of me.
With every princess I had many a tryst,
And every queen came begging to be kissed;
The Ethiopian and the Japanese
Murmured my name in all their sighs and pleas.
Two sultanesses could not but adore me,
Two more escaped from the seraglio fòr me,
Which strained my friendship with the Turkish nation.

CLINDOR

Their anger could but gild your reputation.

MATAMORE

Still, all that was more trouble than it was worth.
It balked my plans for conquering the earth.
What's more, I tired of it, and to deter
Such nuisances sent word to Jupiter
That if he could not put a stop to these
Fond women and their importunities,
I'd rise up in a rage and end his reign
As ruler of the gods, and would obtain
For Mars the right to throw his bolts of thunder.
Needless to say, the coward knuckled under:
He did as I desired, and now, you see,
I'm handsome only when I choose to be.

CLINDOR

What love-notes you'd receive, were that not so!

MATAMORE

Don't bring me any . . . Unless from her, you know.
What does she say of me?

CLINDOR

                    Today she said
That you inspire all hearts with love and dread,
And that if what you promise her comes true,
She'll feel herself a goddess, thanks to you.

MATAMORE

Back in the times I've just been speaking of,
Goddesses, also, pestered me for love,
And I shall tell you of a strange event
Which caused confusion without precedent
And threw all nature into disarray.
The Sun was powerless to rise one day
Because that bright, much-worshiped deity
Could not find where the Dawn, his guide, might be.
He sought her everywhere, in Cephalus's bower,
In old Tithonus's bed, in Memnon's tower,
But since Aurora nowhere was in sight,
The day, till noontide, was as black as night.

CLINDOR

Where was the goddess, during these alarms?

MATAMORE

In my bedchamber, offering me her charms.
But she gained nothing by such shameless actions;
My heart was blind to all her bright attractions,
And all she got by showing off her beauty
Was a firm command to go and do her duty.

CLINDOR

That curious story, Sir, I now recall.
I was in Mexico, where I heard it all.
They said that Persia, vexed by the insult to
Their famous Sun-God, had it in for you.

MATAMORE

I heard as much, and would have made them pay,
But was in Transylvania that day,
Where their ambassador hastened to appease
My wrath with presents and apologies.

CLINDOR

Your brave heart showed them clemency. How fine!

MATAMORE

Just look, my friend, upon this face of mine.
There every human virtue can be found.

Of all the foes I've stamped into the ground,
Whose kingdoms are annulled and cast aside,
There was not one who did not fall through pride.
But those who humbly honored my perfection
Have kept their power through a wise subjection.
The modest kings of Europe are all my vassals;
I do not sack their towns or wreck their castles;
I let them reign. But it's another story
In Africa, where I scorched the territory
Of certain kings who lacked humility,
And left great deserts there for all to see.
Those endless sands, beneath those skies of fire,
Are a great monument to my righteous ire.

CLINDOR

Let us revert to love; your lady's here.

MATAMORE

My cursèd rival's at her side, I fear.

CLINDOR

Where are you going?

MATAMORE

       He isn't brave, this dunce,
And yet he's vain, and could be bold for once.
Perhaps he'll challenge me from foolish pride,
Merely because he's at the lady's side.

CLINDOR

By doing so, the fool might come to harm.

MATAMORE

I can't be valorous when I'm full of charm.

CLINDOR

Cease to be charming and be terrible, Sir.

MATAMORE

Oh, you don't realize what that would incur.
I can't be terrible by halves, you know;
I'd slaughter both my mistress and my foe.
Until they part, let's stand aside and wait.

CLINDOR

Your prudence, like your valor, is very great.
(*They withdraw to a corner.*)

Scene III

ADRASTE

If that's the case, then I must live in pain;
I sigh, I suffer, and it's all in vain.
Despite my fervent declarations, you
Will not believe I love you as I do.

ISABELLE

I don't quite see, Sir, what you're asking of me.
No doubt I'm lovable, and I'm sure you love me.
I know it by your sighs, which are intense,
And even if I lacked that evidence,
I always have, if possible, preferred
To trust a man, and take him at his word.
Pray do the like for me: since I conceal
Nothing from you of what I truly feel,
Kindly believe that though I trust your claim
To love me, Sir, I cannot say the same.

ADRASTE

Ah, cruel one, is this my payment for
The months in which I've been your servitor?

Is faithful love so bad a thing that I'm
Condemned to endless scorn for such a crime?

ISABELLE

We've often differed in the terms we chose:
What I would call a thorn, you call a rose;
What you call faithfulness and constancy
Are persecution and duress to me.
Each clings to his position: you tell me yet
That your dreary courtship puts me in your debt,
And I say that the services you rate
So highly are but grounds for scorn and hate.

ADRASTE

How is it possible that the heaven-born
Passion I feel should merit only scorn?
Yes, heaven, with the first breath that I drew,
Gave me a heart prepared to worship you;
Your image was imprinted on my soul
And, ere I saw you, was its only goal.
When I surrendered to your sweet allures,
I gave you nothing not already yours,
Nothing not meant for you in heaven's plan.

ISABELLE

I wish that heaven had picked some other man.
You're doomed to love me, I to say you nay:
Let's both be careful not to disobey.

Somehow you have invited heaven's hate,
Or there's some crime it bids you expiate,
For I believe no torment is more painful
Than that of loving someone who's disdainful.

ADRASTE

Since what I suffer is so clear to you,
Shall you refuse the pity which is my due?

ISABELLE

Indeed, I pity you, and all the more
Because your sufferings are a useless bore
The only fruit of which, I fear, will be
The record of a joyless constancy.

ADRASTE

Your father backs me, and as things now stand,
What you won't grant I'll ask him to command.

ISABELLE

That's not the way, Sir, to achieve your aim;
Such a fine move can bring you only shame.

ADRASTE

I hope to see, before this day is through,
That what your heart can't say, his will can do.

ISABELLE

I hope to see, before this day is over,
Disaster fall upon a tiresome lover.

ADRASTE

Oh, come now! Will your harshness never cease?

ISABELLE

Go find my father, and leave me here in peace.

ADRASTE

Your heart regrets its coldness in the past,
I think, and needs some force to thaw at last.
I'll go to him at once, and I shall say
That it's your true desires that I obey.

ISABELLE

Go, go, Sir, and pursue your hopeless plan.

Scene IV

MATAMORE

Well! When he saw me, how that coward ran!
Did he not flee, the instant that I came?

ISABELLE

That's no disgrace, Sir; kings have done the same,
If all the glowing rumors that I hear
Of your great deeds do not deceive my ear.

MATAMORE

You may believe them, Madam; and if you'll
Pick out some countries that you'd like to rule,
I'll shape an empire that will please us both.
I swear it by this arm. You have my oath.

ISABELLE

Ah, don't employ that conquering arm in vain;
It's only in your heart that I would reign.
The one ambition that my love inspires
Is to be mistress of your heart's desires.

MATAMORE

And so you are. To show you that my soul
Is absolutely under your control,
I'll think no more of conquest; I'll allow
The world's crowned heads to keep their crowns for now,
Save for a few I'll dress in livery
To bring you billets-doux on bended knee.

ISABELLE

Such regal servants, I'm afraid, would give
Good grounds for envy of the way I live.
For the interchange of our affections, Sir,
We only need our present messenger.
                (She gestures toward Clindor.)

MATAMORE

By heaven, Madam, we see eye to eye:
You have no taste for grandeur, nor do I.
Sceptres are nothing to me; I don't desire them,
And give them back as fast as I acquire them.
Princesses have adored me—there were many—
But never did I give my heart to any.

ISABELLE

Your last assertion strains credulity;
You gave up all those princesses for me,
Refusing them the heart I hold so dear?

MATAMORE

Young Clindor can support my claim. (*To Clindor.*)
    Come here.
In China, at that famous tourney, I
Was seen by the king's two daughters, riding by;
What did you hear about the violent
Infatuation which they underwent?

CLINDOR

Both died of grief, because you spurned them coldly.
It was in Egypt that the news was told me;
There, at that time, your prowess caused such fears
That Cairo was aswim in nervous tears.
You had just slain ten giants in one day,
Laid waste the lands of Caliph and of Bey,
Razed fifteen castles, cut two mountains down,
Applied the torch to forest, field, and town,
And near Damascus killed ten thousand foes.

MATAMORE

You have a splendid memory, heaven knows.
I had forgotten.

ISABELLE

    How could it slip your mind
That you'd done deeds of such a glorious kind?

MATAMORE

My memory's full of laurels wrenched from kings:
I don't encumber it with lesser things.

Scene V

PAGE

Sir.

MATAMORE

Well, what is it, page?

PAGE

A courier.

MATAMORE

Who sent him here?

PAGE

The Queen of Iceland, Sir.

MATAMORE

Great God! That queen's become a dreadful pest.
Less charm is what I need, and a little rest.
Let her forget me, as I've told her to.

CLINDOR

See what this warrior's given up for you?

ISABELLE

I doubt no longer.

CLINDOR

It's just as he described.

MATAMORE

In vain she tempts me; I will not be bribed.
Whatever foolish plans are in her head,
I'll write a letter which will stop them dead.
Farewell, my queen. Meanwhile, do lend an ear
To the conversation of my young friend here;
He knows my life, and could tell you hour by hour
What sort of man you hold now in your power.

ISABELLE

Don't stay away too long, Sir. I shall learn
Your love for me by the speed of your return.

Scene VI

CLINDOR

His character is what you should assess:
He keeps that page from sheer pretentiousness—
To tell Milord from time to time that some
Ambassador or messenger has come.

ISABELLE

I liked that message far more than he knew:
It rid me of a fool, and left me you.

CLINDOR

Those words of yours embolden me to make
Use of this moment for confession's sake.

ISABELLE

What's your confession?

CLINDOR

That I love Isabelle
With heart and soul, and more than I can tell;
That I adore . . .

ISABELLE

No need to talk that way;
I know it's true; what more is there to say?
I spurn a diadem, by reason òf you,
I scorn your rival and, in short, I love you.
Uncertain lovers, with their flimsy passion,
Proclaim their feelings in a wordy fashion;
For us, it's moments such as this that matter;
One glance, for us, says more than all their chatter.

CLINDOR

Who would have dreamt that cruel fate could start
To smile, like this, on my enraptured heart!
Driven by a father's rigor from my home,
Obliged, in friendless poverty, to roam
Until engaged to flatter every whim
Of a mad master, and kowtow to him—
Somehow, my sorry history does not
Disgust you with the meanness of my lot,
And a rival's wealth and station matter less
To you than my sincere devotedness.

ISABELLE

That's how the heart should choose. True love is drawn
Toward what is sweet to look and think upon.
To think as well of money or position,
Thus mingling love with avarice and ambition,
Is but defilement and a wretched stain
On the noblest dream our spirits can attain.

My father will have other plans, and he
Will seek to bar us from felicity;
But love has such a hold upon my soul
That I'll no longer yield to his control.
My father's choice for me he shan't enforce;
Whatever he wishes, I shall choose my course.

CLINDOR

Unworthy as I am, it staggers me . . .

ISABELLE

Here comes my pesterer, and I must flee.

Scene VII

ADRASTE

How fortunate you are, how luckless I!
My lady likes you; my coming makes her fly.
She somehow finds your company to her taste,
But when I came in sight, she left in haste.

CLINDOR

She didn't see you coming into view
When, weary of my talk, she said adieu.

ADRASTE

What? Weary of your talk? It's curious for
A bright, attractive man to be a bore.
What were you speaking of that wearied her?

CLINDOR

Oh, things that you might easily infer:
My master's fancied love-affairs, his dreams
Of martial glory, and related themes.

ADRASTE

Do me a service. Neither you nor he
Could give me any cause for jealousy;
But if you can't rein in his fantasies,
Try to direct them elsewhere, if you please.

CLINDOR

How can you fear a man who, courting her,
Speaks not of love, but sack and massacre,
And how he likes to hack, burn, slash, and slay?

ADRASTE

You're not the type, I think, for a valet.
How can you serve, unless for secret gain,
A braggart madder than his boasts are vain?
In any case, since she's been seeing you,
She's been more cold to me than hitherto:
Either you're someone's agent, or you bank
On projects not consistent with your rank.
I don't doubt that you're up to something shady.
So: bid your master find some other lady;
Or if he will not do so, tell him to
Employ some other go-between than you.
Her father, to be sure, will soon take action
And settle matters to my satisfaction,
But meanwhile, ease my mind of this small worry,
And if you love your life, leave in a hurry;

For if you dare come through that door again,
I well know how to deal with shady men.

CLINDOR

Do you think I stand between you and her hand?

ADRASTE

I want no back-talk, do you understand?
Be off with you.

CLINDOR

On mere suspicion, you
Should not insult a brave man as you do.
I was not born the lord of any manor,
But heaven gave me heart, and a sense of honor,
And I shall settle all accounts some day.

ADRASTE

You threaten me?

CLINDOR

No, no; I'm on my way.
Your cruel insult will bear bitter fruit,
But this is not the place for a dispute.

Scene VIII

ADRASTE, LYSE

ADRASTE

That insolent reprobate defies me still.

LYSE

If that's what's eating you, I think you're ill.

ADRASTE

You think I'm ill?

LYSE

I do; you're jealous, Sir,
Of the hireling of a half-mad posturer.

ADRASTE

I know my rank, and Isabelle's. There's no way
That I could lose her hand to some valet.
Nevertheless it vexes me that she
Should take such pleasure in his company.

LYSE

In short, Sir, you are of two minds precisely.

ADRASTE

Say, if you like, that I've behaved unwisely,
That my suspicions are or are not blind:
I sent him packing for my peace of mind.
But what, in fact, is going on?

LYSE

                              Oh, well:
The truth is that he's loved by Isabelle.

ADRASTE

What are you saying, Lyse?

LYSE

                              That they belong
To one another; that their love is strong;
That they are burning with a single flame.

ADRASTE

Ungrateful, treacherous woman! Ah, for shame!
You dare prefer a common rogue to me?

LYSE

There's no end to the rogue's effrontery,
And let me tell you that his latest whim
Is that he's rich and noble.

ADRASTE

The nerve of him!

LYSE

His father's strictness made him run away,
And so he variously went astray
Until, from want or whim, he settled for
The service of our warrior Matamore.
Pretending to advance his master's suit,
He proved himself ingenious and astute,
Enchanting the deluded lady who,
Despite your ardor, now refuses you.
But if you speak now to her father, Sir,
He soon will teach obedience to her.

ADRASTE

He's just assured me that my faithfulness
Is to be crowned with a deserved success,
And that her hand will soon be given tò me.
But wait; there's one more favor you can do me.

LYSE

I'm at your service; what favor do you mean?

ADRASTE

Help me surprise them in an amorous scene.

LYSE

That's easy. Tonight, perhaps, you'll have your cue.

ADRASTE

Farewell. Remember, help me catch those two.
Meanwhile, accept this as a small advance.
>   (*He drops something into her hand.*)

LYSE

I hope your cane will make that rascal dance!

ADRASTE

I promise you that there will be no lack
Of wood unloaded on that fellow's back.

Scene IX

LYSE

Although that proud fop thinks he's won the prize, he
Will find it wasn't prudent to despise me.
He's vain of his good looks, and looks with scorn
On any girl who isn't nobly born.
I don't deserve his kisses, I'm afraid:
His taste is for the mistress, not the maid.
I'm just a servant; but what is he, the cad?
His face is pretty, but mine is not too bad.
He's rich and noble; that's his crazy claim;
So far from home, who couldn't say the same?
In any case, tonight Sir Noble Riches
Will dance, while a cane beats time upon his breeches.

Scene X

ALCANDRE

Your heart is pounding.

PRIDAMANT

Yes, I feel alarm.

ALCANDRE

Lyse loves Clindor too much to do him harm.

PRIDAMANT

He scorned her, and she has revenge in mind.

ALCANDRE

Don't worry; love will move her to be kind.

ACT III

Scene I

GÉRONTE

Restrain those sighs and dry that tearful cheek;
Against my will, such weaponry is weak;
My heart, though touched by your distress, adheres
To reason, and will not be moved by tears.
I know what's good for you. You take a dim
View of Adraste because I favor him,
And since I'd have you marry him, your pride
Thinks him unfit to claim you as his bride.
Come! What do you think he lacks—wealth, rank, or
       bravery?
Is it his looks or soul you find unsavory?
You should feel honored . . .

ISABELLE

                        He's perfect, and I know
I should be happier to be honored so;
But if you'll let me, with all deference,
Venture a word or two in my defense,
There's a deep instinct in me, Sir, which can
Admire Adraste, but cannot love the man.
Sometimes, I know not how, we are inspired

By heaven to resist what is desired,
And not to be obedient, though pressed,
When what's been chosen for us, we detest.
The souls which, here below, are linked by love
Were destined to be so by heaven above;
Those who ignore that guidance are misled,
And those who wed without it are not wed.
To go against what heaven's laws dispense,
And doubt the wisdom of such providence,
Is to rebel, and to invite the dire
Results which come of rousing heaven's ire.

GÉRONTE

Is this, girl, how you dare to answer me?
What teacher taught you that philosophy?
You've learned your lessons very well, but still
Your fine ideas won't overcome my will.
If heaven makes you view my choice with hate,
Is that bold warrior your candidate?
Has that great conqueror enslaved your soul,
Just as he's tamed the cosmos as a whole?
Shall a mad braggart grace our family tree?

ISABELLE

Spare me that fate, Sir. It's my earnest plea!

GÉRONTE

Then why you won't obey me I can't guess.

ISABELLE

My peace of mind, Sir, and my happiness.
The brilliant match you favor I would find
A joyless hell in which I was confined.

GÉRONTE

Ha! Prettier girls than you are, Isabelle,
Would be content to live in such a hell!
Enough; give in, and yield to my behest.

ISABELLE

Put my obedience to some other test.

GÉRONTE

From now on, I've no wish to be defied.
We've argued for the last time. Go inside.

Scene II

The young, these days, begrudge us their submission,
And duty seems to them an imposition.
Prerogatives of the most sacred kind
Can't overcome their stubbornness of mind.
Young girls, particularly, balk at our
Authority and our paternal power,
Persist in their caprices, contradict,
And do not like the husbands we have picked.
However, have no hopes, my little hellion,
That my wise plans will yield to your rebellion.
        (*He sees Matamore approaching.*)
But here's that madman back again, and I'll
Get rid of him, I swear, by force or guile.

Scene III

MATAMORE (*To Clindor.*)

Do I not have a difficult existence?
The Grand Vizier asks once more for assistance,
Tartary begs me to unsheathe my blade,
Cathay and Calicut implore my aid:
What can I do? Divide myself in four?

CLINDOR

I'd let them go, without your help, to war:
For if you helped but one, there would be three
Disgruntled and consumed with jealousy.

MATAMORE

Quite right; enough of warfare. Only in love
Would I be someone to be jealous of.
(*To Géronte.*)
Ah, Sir, you must forgive me. Near as we were,
I didn't bow, for I failed to see you, Sir.
But what is this upon your face? A frown?
Where are your enemies? Let me mow them down.

GÉRONTE

Thanks be to God, I have no enemies.

MATAMORE

Thanks to this arm, which forced them to their knees!

GÉRONTE

Of that good deed I'd not been notified.

MATAMORE

When they perceived that I was on your side,
They all were paralyzed, or died of fear.

GÉRONTE

You should be somewhere else these days, not here.
In a time of many wars, your famous arm
Should be in action, doing dreadful harm.
Strolling the pavements of a peaceful town
Is not the way to burnish your renown.
People begin to be a lot less awed,
And some regard you as a swaggering fraud.

MATAMORE

Zounds! What you say could not be truer, Sir,
But how can I leave when I'm a prisoner?
Isabelle's charms, which can but be adored,
Detain me here, and make me sheathe my sword.

GÉRONTE

If it is only she who holds you back,
Feel free to gather up your things and pack.
She's not for you; it's time you left the scene.

MATAMORE

Zounds! What have you said? I want her for my queen.

GÉRONTE

I'm not in the mood to laugh again while you
Recite preposterous tales of derring-do.
Old jokes, repeated, do not please so well.
Go, find some other queen than Isabelle,
And if you dare come courting her again . . .

MATAMORE

He speaks to me like that! The man's insane.
Do you not know that mention of me makes
The Great Turk flee, and devils have the shakes?
That in a flash I could abolish you?

GÉRONTE

Here in my house I have some servants who,
Though not your match for braggadocio,
Could answer you with many a solid blow.

MATAMORE (*To Clindor.*)

Tell him the thousand things that I have done.

GÉRONTE

Be modest, Sir. It's best in the long run.
Good-bye. Though not your enemy, let me say
That I'm quick to act, and my servants to obey.

Scene IV

MATAMORE

Respect for my beloved hampers me;
My rage is sacrificed to gallantry.
Would that I faced a hundred foemen rather
Than one I cannot kill—my lady's father!
Ah, fiend incarnate, scrawny apparition,
Old imp of Satan, image of perdition,
How dare you banish me, and slight thereby
One for whose favor kings and popes apply?

CLINDOR

While he is gone, Sir, go in while you can
And see your queen, despite his foolish ban.

MATAMORE

Alack! His servants might try something rough.

CLINDOR

That sword of yours would tame them soon enough.

MATAMORE

Yes, but my sword, when drawn, throws off such fire
As could in moments burn the house entire,
Devouring in a flash the slates and gutters,
The beams and braces, rafters, panes, and shutters,
The posts and purlins, columns, jambs, and sills,
Joists, lintels, girders, copings, rails, and grilles,
The tiles, the stones, the locks and bolts and doors,
Iron, plaster, marble, glass, the oaken floors,
Cellars and attics, closets, rooms and halls,
Stairways and landings, and at last the walls.
Just think how my enchantress would respond
To that; her heart no longer would be fond.
Go pay her my respects; since you're not such
A threat as I, the servants won't do much.

CLINDOR

They won't?

MATAMORE

That door is opening, I see.
Good-bye. Those lackeys might be rude to me.

Scene V

CLINDOR (*Alone.*)

That champion coward can be made afraid
By a trembling leaf, a vapor, or a shade!
Old men can scare him, a girl can make him run,
And fear of a thrashing has him quite undone.
(*To Lyse.*)
Lyse, your entrance was enough to start
A sudden panic in the noble heart
Of that bold hero, that knight of dauntless mien,
Who conquers kings and dazzles many a queen.

LYSE

Some faces, even from afar, can charm;
Mine, at close range, appears to cause alarm.

CLINDOR

Well, if it frightens fools, it charms the wise:
Few faces are so fetching, in my eyes.
If men adore you, they have reason to;
I've never seen a prettier girl than you—
Good-natured, sprightly, with a bantering wit,
The bosom full, the figure exquisite,

Bright eyes, fine features, and the cheeks aglow—
Who wouldn't love you, I should like to know?

LYSE

Since when have I been so beautiful? Look well:
I'm Lyse, after all, not Isabelle.

CLINDOR

You two have equal shares in my affections.
I worship both her wealth and your perfections.

LYSE

I fear that my perfections must concede
The match to wealth. One love is all you need.

CLINDOR

I'll do my best to marry her, that's true,
But does that mean I love her more than you?
Marriage and love have different goals in sight:
One's for convenience, the other for delight.
I'm penniless, and so you, too, must be;
Two zeros, Lyse, equal poverty,
And though, at first, love makes for sunny weather,
There's little joy in being poor together.
So I court someone else for money's sake,
But cannot look at you without an ache
Of longing, and a heartfelt sigh because
My heart is stifled by my reason's laws.

To your least glance, my spirit is in thrall;
Ah! How I'd love you, if to love were all.
And how you'd please me if I had my wish!

LYSE

How wise you'd be, if you talked less gibberish,
Or saved at least until a better season
Such eloquence regarding love and reason!
How fine to have a swain who, from a sort
Of strange compassion, does not pay me court,
But seeks another woman for his wife
To spare me an impoverished married life!
I shan't forget your noble qualities.
Go now and pay your visit, if you please.

CLINDOR

I'd be far happier if I didn't leave you.

LYSE

My mistress waits below and will receive you.

CLINDOR

You drive me off!

LYSE

I'm sending you where your
Felicity's more likely to endure.

CLINDOR

Ah! You're enchanting even in disdain.

LYSE

You're wasting precious time if you remain.

CLINDOR

Remember, if I court another, it's—

LYSE

For fear of joining our two deficits.
You've said that once, and I shall not forget.

CLINDOR

Your sharp wit makes you more attractive yet.
Farewell: each minute, your appeal is stronger,
And, if I could, I'd love to tarry longer.

Scene VI

LYSE

The scoundrel finally takes notice òf me,
And to amuse himself pretends to love me!
Blind to my feelings, he now pays me court
With clever compliments all made in sport,
And with an instant infidelity
Swears he adores me and wants none of me.
Love left and right, you villain, divide your heart,
Pick out your wife or mistress à la carte,
Let interest govern all you feel or do,
But don't think that we won't be on to you!
A scheming heart's not worthy of Isabelle,
And such a lover wouldn't suit me well.
I joked with you, but only to conceal
From you the sharp resentment that I feel.
Had I shown rage, you might then have divined
The well-deserved revenge I have in mind,
But my pretense of sweetness has prepared
The trap in which you soon will be ensnared.
And yet, in truth, how wicked have you been?
To seek one's fortune—is that such a sin?
You love me, yet you yield to money's claim:
Who, in this century, would not do the same?
Forget what self-contempt he should confess,

And let him have his share of happiness.
If he loves me, he can't mean to do me ill,
And I should spare him, if I love him still.
Lord! How have I drifted into such a mood?
How can I pardon an affront so rude?
My just desire for vengeance—how can I
Abandon it, and let my anger die?
He loves me, and he seeks another bride.
I love him, and he brushes me aside!
Enough of love, my heart, it's time for hate.
I swear it, and I shall not vacillate:
Your softness has but made my pain the greater;
Give up your sweetness now, and be a hater.
It's hatred's turn to rule my spirit, for
When love's been wronged, it should be love no more.

Scene VII

MATAMORE

They're coming. I must escape. No, no one's here.
Go forward, then. My body shakes with fear.
I hear them. No, it's just the wind. All right—
Move swiftly under cover of the night.
Old fool, despite you I shall court my queen!
Those lackeys have me feeling faint and green.
I've never trembled so, upon my honor.
The risk's too great; if they see me, I'm a goner,
For if they dared attack, I'd rather die
Than soil this arm by fighting such *canaille*.
What perils does our valor make us face!
Well, I am fleet of foot, in any case;
If I had to run, I'd put them in the shade.
My foot is even quicker than my blade.
But now, for sure, they're coming. I'm dead, I'm done.
My body's frozen and I cannot run.
O Fate, how harsh you are and how contràry!
Ah! It's my lady and my secretary.
I'll hide and listen, while my terror thaws,
And see how well he pleads my amorous cause.

Scene VIII

CLINDOR, MATAMORE, ISABELLE

ISABELLE

I'm troubled by my father's attitude;
I've never seen him in so fierce a mood.
You and your master are denied our door.
Your rival's in a jealous rage, what's more.
That's why we meet down here; 'twould mean our doom
If they surprised us in an upper room.
Here we may talk in peace and feel no worry;
You have two doors for leaving in a hurry,
And if they came I could withdraw with ease.

CLINDOR

Don't fret too much about my safety, please.

ISABELLE

How could I be too careful of a prize
To which all else is nothing in my eyes,
A prize that's life itself to me, that's worth
Whatever I esteem in all the earth?
A rival, backed by Father, seeks my hand
And heart—which you, you only, shall command.

I'm constantly tormented by those two,
Yet I rejoice in suffering for you,
And count as blessèd every pang or ache
That I must undergo for your dear sake.

CLINDOR

I'm overwhelmed; and in return, I fear,
All I can offer is my life; for here
My lifeblood, which I'd gladly shed for you,
Is the one possession I have title to.
But if, some day, my stars look kindlier down,
And let me see once more my native town,
You'll learn that he you've chosen is not base,
And that my rival's of no nobler race.
Yet, happy as I am, I worry still
Lest father and rival should impose their will.

ISABELLE

Believe me, you've no reason for alarm.
One has less power than the other charm.
I shall not tell you what resolve I've made;
Suffice to say that I shall not be swayed,
And that their schemes are therefore vain and weak.
I promise—

MATAMORE

I can't bear this; I must speak.

ISABELLE

Gods! Someone's heard us.

CLINDOR

       Our martial friend, no doubt.
I'll calm him down; there's nothing to fret about.

Scene IX

MATAMORE

You traitor!

CLINDOR

Hush; the servants . . .

MATAMORE

What do you mean?

CLINDOR

Might fall upon us if we're heard or seen.

MATAMORE (*Drawing Clindor to
one corner of the stage.*)

Come here. You know what treachery you've shown.
You haven't pled my suit. You've pled your own.

CLINDOR

I sought for happiness, I can't deny.

MATAMORE

You have a choice of several ways to die.
I'll shatter you like glass, instanter, or
I'll thrust you living to the earth's hot core,
Or make you mincemeat with one backhand blow,
Or fling you skyward with so great a throw
That elemental fire will shrivel you.
Choose quickly, rogue. And say your prayers, too.

CLINDOR

Now *you* shall choose.

MATAMORE

What am I to decide?

CLINDOR

Either you leave or I shall flay your hide.

MATAMORE

He threatens me! What presumption, if you please!
When he should beg my pardon on his knees! . . .
He and those lackeys are in league . . . I'll call
On the seven seas to rise and drown you all.

CLINDOR

A smaller grave will serve for you, I think.
I'll throw you in the river and watch you sink.

MATAMORE

They're hand in glove! I knew it!

CLINDOR

                    Hush, blatherskite:
I have already killed ten men tonight,
And if you vex me I'll extend my string.

MATAMORE

By God! This rogue has been beneath my wing,
And learned from me how brave men talk and act.
I'd like the fellow if he showed more tact.
See here: I'm lenient; it would be too bad
To cheat the universe of so brave a lad.
Just ask my pardon, and profane no more
By your attentions her whom I adore.
You know my valor; accept my clemency.

CLINDOR

Well, since you love so fiercely, why don't we
Cross swords a bit and see who wins the day?

MATAMORE

I'm charmed by the noble spirit you display.
Enough. She's yours, dear boy, as a reward
For the faithful services which you afford.
Don't ever say you had a thankless master!

CLINDOR

This wondrous present makes my heart beat faster.
O generous warrior, prop of many a king,
Through all creation may your praises ring!

Scene X

ISABELLE

I thank the heavens that this meeting ends
Without a fight, and that you two are friends.

MATAMORE

My queen, you must no longer think that I
Will claim your hand in marriage by and by;
For various reasons, there's a change of plan.
But let me offer you another man:
He, too, is brave, and you'll think highly òf him;
He served with me.

ISABELLE

To please you, I shall love him.

CLINDOR

But keep the secret, Sir, of our affection.

MATAMORE

I promise you both silence and protection.
Wherever you go, you've but to mention me.

I'm dreaded equally on land and sea.
Go now; a happy marriage to you both.

ISABELLE

As you suggest, I pledge to him my troth.

CLINDOR

Now bid her give me, as my future wife—

Scene XI

GÉRONTE, ADRASTE, MATAMORE, CLINDOR,
ISABELLE, LYSE, AND A NUMBER OF SERVANTS

ADRASTE

Those insolent words, you knave, will cost your life!

MATAMORE

They've caught my courage napping. Ah, that door
Is open; I shall climb to the upper floor.
(*He goes into Isabelle's room, following her and Lyse.*)

CLINDOR

Villain! You've come protected by a throng
Of thugs, but I shall pick you out ere long.

GÉRONTE

Adraste is wounded! Run for the doctor, do.
And seize that murderer, the rest of you.

CLINDOR

I yield, outnumbered. Dearest Isabelle,
Fate hurls me from a precipice. Farewell.

GÉRONTE

He breathes no more. Come, bear his corpse away.
You, take that knave to prison, without delay.

Scene XII

PRIDAMANT

Alas, my son is dead!

ALCANDRE

Feel no alarm.

PRIDAMANT

Can you not save him with some magic charm?

ALCANDRE

No need of that. Be patient, and you shall see
Your son made happy by love's alchemy.

ACT IV

Scene I

The end is near. A venal magistrate
Shall rule tomorrow that we must immolate
My lover to the villain who was bent
On killing him. It's revenge, not punishment.
Tomorrow, by a harsh, unjust decree,
My father's hate shall gain the victory,
Together with the dead man's wealth and station,
And I shall know despair and desolation.
Alas! How many strong and bitter foes
Assail his helpless innocence, and oppose
A poor young man whose only crime could be
That he dared love me, and was loved by me.
Yes, Clindor, that high passion which could win
My favor constitutes your only sin.
But I'll not care for life, once you are gone;
I cannot lose my love and yet live on:
I, too, am sentenced by our cruel laws;
I'll share your death, of which I am the cause,
And our two souls will, having died for love,
Be reunited in the realms above.
Thus, Father, you'll be disappointed by
The happy union of our hearts on high,
And if your sorrow at my loss is deep,

My lover and I will laugh to see you weep.
Whatever tears remorse will make you shed
Will add to our delight, and if your dread
And guilty torment are too little still,
I'll haunt you daily, giving you a chill,
I'll dog your footsteps in the dark of night,
Present a thousand horrors to your sight,
Plunge you into an everlasting gloom,
Reproach you for my fate, invite your doom,
And so afflict you, while you gasp for breath,
That you will come to envy me my death.

Scene II

LYSE

Well! Everyone's asleep, but you're awake.
The master's very worried for your sake.

ISABELLE

Lyse, when hope is gone, one has no fear.
It comforts me to vent my sorrows here.
'Twas here that I first saw Clindor's dear face;
His voice still seems to echo in this place,
And here my shattered soul can best recover
The dear remembered presence of my lover.

LYSE

How busily you work at being grieved.

ISABELLE

What else should I be doing, thus bereaved?

LYSE

There were two sterling men you might have wed;
One dies tomorrow, and one's already dead.

Go find a living one, and we'll see whether
He isn't worth the first two put together.

ISABELLE

How dare you say to me so crass a thing?

LYSE

What good is all your useless whimpering?
D'you think that tears, which spoil your looks, will save
Your lover from the gallows and the grave?
Think rather of how to make a brilliant match;
I know a man who'd be a splendid catch,
And he admires you, too.

ISABELLE

           Get out of my sight.

LYSE

Truly, no other choice could be so right.

ISABELLE

Must you torment me? How can you do this tò me?

LYSE

Must I conceal my joy because you're gloomy?

ISABELLE

What joy is this, that comes so out of season?

LYSE

Once I've explained, you'll say that I've good reason.

ISABELLE

No. Spare me.

LYSE

This concerns you, or it will.

ISABELLE

Speak only of Clindor, or else be still.

LYSE

My cheerful nature, which laughs when life is trying,
Does more in minutes than an age of crying.
It's saved Clindor.

ISABELLE

It's saved Clindor?

LYSE

Yes, he.
May that convince you of my loyalty.

ISABELLE

Oh, please, please tell me where to go. Where is he?

LYSE

I've but begun things. You must now get busy.

ISABELLE

Oh, Lyse!

LYSE

You'd fly with him? You feel no doubt?

ISABELLE

Not follow one I cannot live without?
Lyse, if you can't free him from his cell,
I'll join him even in the depths of hell.
Don't ask again if I shall cleave to him.

LYSE

Since love has given you a resolve so grim,
Hear what I've done, then do what you must do.
If he doesn't escape, the fault will lie with you.
The prison's near at hand.

ISABELLE

Yes?

LYSE

And that is why
The jailer's brother has seen me walking by:
And, since to see me is to love me, he—
Poor devil—has quite lost his heart to me.

ISABELLE

You never told me!

LYSE

I could not admit
What would have shamed me had you heard of it;
But since Clindor's arrest four days ago
I have been kinder to my simple beau,
Letting him think, by many a word or glance,
That he and I are having a romance.
When a man believes that we reciprocate
His love, it puts him in a docile state;
That's how I got a purchase on his soul,
And moved him to submit to my control.
Once he believed I might be his for life,
I said I couldn't be a jailer's wife.
He said it was a dismal trade, but it
Would be extremely hard, he said, to quit,
Since, save for locks and cells, there was no other
Good livelihood for him and for his brother.
At once I told him that he couldn't be
More blest with luck and opportunity;

That if he'd only do as I had planned,
He'd soon grow rich and so could ask my hand;
That a Breton noble was detained by him
Who used Sir Delamont as a pseudonym;
That we must free him, see him home, and thus
Secure a patron who'd be good to us.
My beau was staggered; I pressed him; he declined;
He spoke of love; I'd other things in mind;
I left in anger; distressed, he followed then
And made excuses; I refused again.

ISABELLE

And?

LYSE

The next day he seemed shaken; I insisted
Once more upon my plan, but he resisted.
I said this morning, "This is the crucial day;
You're free to act; your brother is away."
He said, "But we need money to equip
Ourselves for such a long and costly trip.
The gentleman hasn't any."

ISABELLE

Lyse, you ought
To have given him, without a moment's thought,
My pearls, my rings, my all.

LYSE

I told him, too,
That his noble prisoner was in love with you,
And you with him, and that you'd flee with us.
At these words he grew sweet and ceased to fuss,
Which made me realize that he'd had, before,
A foolish jealousy of your Clindor,
And so had balked for fear that he'd discover,
On freeing him, that Clindor was my lover.
Knowing the truth now, he was quick to shape
Our plans and preparations for escape,
And bade me tell you that at twelve tonight
You must be ready for our secret flight.

ISABELLE

How many thanks I owe you!

LYSE

Pray add one more;
By marrying a man I find a bore
I sacrifice myself to your content.

ISABELLE

My dear—

LYSE

I want no thanks. It's time you went
To pack your luggage; and, before we dash,

Add to your jewelry the old man's cash.
I'll let you have his treasures very cheap—
I stole his key-ring once he'd gone to sleep.
Here, take it.

ISABELLE

Let's do the job together.

LYSE

No,

Do it without me.

ISABELLE

What! Does it scare you so?

LYSE

No, but we'd wake him up. That's a sure thing.
We couldn't keep ourselves from chattering.

ISABELLE

You crazy girl.

LYSE

Lest there be any slip,
I'll wait here for the leader of our trip;
If he were seen outside, it wouldn't do.
As soon as he comes, we'll give the word to you.
Be serious, now.

ISABELLE

I'm on my way. Farewell.
I'll let you be the mistress for a spell.

LYSE

That's only right.

ISABELLE

Be watchful.

LYSE

Fill your purse.

Scene III

Clindor, I'm both your blessing and your curse.
I gave you chains, I free you now, and I
Still have the power to make you live or die.
My vengeance went much farther than I'd meant;
Merely to chasten you was my intent.
Your too-harsh fate has made me change my mind;
I wish you life, and joy of every kind;
Your plight has made my love revive, and made
Me spurn revenge and hasten to your aid.
I hope you, too, Clindor, will rise above
Your former selfish and philandering love.

Scene IV

MATAMORE, ISABELLE, LYSE

ISABELLE

What! Here? At night?

MATAMORE

The other day—

ISABELLE

Be clear.
"The other day," you say, and you're still here?

LYSE

Well, well! You've found the stalwart captain! Where?

ISABELLE

I just now met him, coming down the stair.

MATAMORE

The other day, in lieu of my affection,
I promised you, dear lady, my protection.

ISABELLE

And then?

MATAMORE

Some rascals then began to brawl,
You sought your quarters to avoid it all,
And, to protect you, I came close behind.

ISABELLE

You had my safety fearlessly in mind.
Then what?

MATAMORE

So as to guard your person well,
I climbed to the top floor as your sentinel.

ISABELLE

And stayed there?

MATAMORE

Yes.

LYSE

In terms less diplomatic,
I'd say you fled in terror to the attic.

MATAMORE

Terror?

LYSE

Yes, fear. Your trembling's obvious.

MATAMORE

Fear is my warhorse, my Bucephalus.
It gives me speed, I've trained it rigorously,
And when I move, it trembles under me.

LYSE

You make a very curious choice of steeds.

MATAMORE

So as to ride full tilt toward glorious deeds.

ISABELLE

Such mastery of fear deserves high praise.
But tell me: were you up there four whole days?

MATAMORE

Four days.

ISABELLE

And what did you eat?

MATAMORE

Ambrosia. Nectar.

ISABELLE

And did that diet pall on my protector?

MATAMORE

No, no.

ISABELLE

But now you've come downstairs at length . . .

MATAMORE

To rescue your beloved, and by my strength
Shatter his prison, and like mighty Mars
Smash into bits his shackles and his bars.

LYSE

Why not admit that you came down instead
To make a sneak attack upon some bread?

MATAMORE

That, too. Ambrosia's more than I can take.
One day of it, and I've a stomachache.
It's a dainty dish, but can't keep one alive.
On such a diet, only gods could thrive.
Just take one bite of it, and in two winks
The teeth grow longer and the belly shrinks.

LYSE

In short, ambrosia's not your cup of tea.

MATAMORE

And so I've come downstairs each night to see
What scraps the kitchen offered, and combine
Some human nutriment with the divine.

ISABELLE

So: you were on your way to steal, just now?

MATAMORE

Dare you insult me, and provoke a row?
If ever I gave vent to rage, I fear—

ISABELLE

Please call my father's servants, Lyse dear.

MATAMORE

Only a fool would linger.

Scene V

LYSE

He got away.

ISABELLE

Well, fear's a racehorse, as we heard him say.

LYSE

But meanwhile you've got little or nothing done.

ISABELLE

Because of him, my packing's not begun.

LYSE

All that you had to do was let him be.

ISABELLE

He recognized me, Lyse, and spoke to me.
Alone at night, I feared his insolence,
Or that some loud discussion might commence
And so, to rid myself of him and fear,

It seemed the wisest thing to bring him here.
Please notice that, with your support, I can
Bravely confront so violent a man.

LYSE

Though I shared your laughter, I also cursed a bit.
What a waste of time!

ISABELLE

I shall make up for it.

LYSE

Here comes the leader of our exodus.
Let's see what plans he has devised for us.

Scene VI

ISABELLE

Well, my good friend, is it time to brave the Fates?
And is it life or death, Sir, that awaits?
It is on you alone my hopes must rest.

JAILER

Banish your fears; all's worked out for the best.
I've horses for you, and I know the route,
And very soon you'll be beyond pursuit.

ISABELLE

You are a guardian angel, in my view;
How shall I find a fit reward for you?

JAILER (*Pointing to Lyse.*)

This is the only prize that I require.

ISABELLE

Then, Lyse, give this man his heart's desire.

LYSE

But can it work, this plan he advocates?
How can we open up the city's gates?

JAILER

Our mounts are waiting just outside of town.
I know a stretch of wall that's falling down,
And we can clamber through the gap with ease.

ISABELLE

Oh! I'm on tenterhooks. Let's hurry, please.

JAILER

Indeed we must.

ISABELLE

But first let's go by stealth
Upstairs, and filch a bit of Father's wealth.

Scene VII

O happy memories of love's delight—
Which soon must yield to suffering—how, despite
Impending horrors and my mortal fear,
Your charming voice still murmurs in my ear!
Do not forsake me, pray possess my mind
In place of matters cruel and unkind;
And when dark visions of mortality
Arise, and thoughts of what's in store for me,
Remind my soul, so troubled and unnerved,
How I've been happier than I deserved.
When I lament the law's severity,
Recall my rashness and temerity;
Tell me that I aspired beyond my place;
That my desire was wrong, my motives base;
That, courting her, I was a miscreant,
Whose death shall be a fitting punishment.
Yet, at my life's end all seems good and right!
Sweet Isabelle, I die your faithful knight,
And whatsoever lance may run me through,
My death is glorious since I die for you.
Alas! How I delude myself, pretending
That to be hanged is not a shameful ending!
And what worse agony than to be denied

Those charms for which I'll be so "glorified"?
There is a murderer's ghost from which I flee;
Alive, he perished; dead, he murders me.
His name does what his sword could not devise;
From where he fell, a thousand murderers rise,
And his spilt blood, on which great falsehoods feed,
Rouses against me an impassioned breed
Who, clothing in the law their bitter hate,
Shall gladly see me murdered by the state.
Tomorrow, I'll be condemned for being brave,
My head shall be awarded to a knave,
And public feeling will permit no doubt
Of how the court's decision must come out.
On all sides, then, my doom's a certainty;
I fought off death, and death's my penalty.
I shall have faced two killers, as it were—
My rival, and then my executioner.
I shudder, thinking thoughts of deepest black;
Even at rest, I am upon the rack;
At midnight, when sweet sleep should seal my eyes,
I see the timbers of my scaffold rise;
The hangman and his gloomy crew appear;
The court's death-sentence thunders in my ear;
I walk with shackled feet; I hear the loud
And vengeful voices of a gathering crowd;
The place where I shall die now comes in sight;
My reason clouds, my soul recoils in fright;
No hope remains, no help is glimpsed ahead;
From fear of death I am already dead.
You only, Isabelle, can rid me of

These terrors by awakening my love;
When your divine perfections come before
My eyes, grim visions frighten me no more.
However fate may deal with me, if then
You will remember me, I shall live again.
But what are you doing here, my friend? Pray tell
Why, at this hour, you unlock my cell.

Scene VIII

JAILER (*While Isabelle and Lyse are seen to one side.*)

The judges of your case, in leniency,
Have issued a compassionate decree.

CLINDOR

Good God! I'm spared?

JAILER

Yes. You shall die at night.

CLINDOR

If that's compassion, what would they do in spite?

JAILER

Be grateful for their kindly resolution:
You're spared the shame of public execution.

CLINDOR

How shall I thank these ministers of death
Who spare and slaughter me in the same breath?

JAILER

You ought to show more gratitude than that.

CLINDOR

Friend, do your duty. I don't care to chat.

JAILER

A band of archers waits for you outside.
Once you have seen them, you'll be mollified.

Scene IX

ISABELLE (*To Lyse, while the jailer is releasing Clindor from prison.*)

Lyse, we'll see him soon!

LYSE

How glad you sound!

ISABELLE

Why not? My life was lost, and now is found.
His fate and mine are partners, side by side,
And I should have to perish if he died.

JAILER

Do you know many archers, Sir, like this?

CLINDOR

Oh, Isabelle, is it you? My God, what bliss!
Good trickster, when you said I'd die at night
You spoke the truth. I'm dying of delight.

ISABELLE

Clindor!

JAILER

Let's have no amorous delays.
We'll soon have time to kiss our fiancées.

CLINDOR

What! You're engaged to Lyse?

ISABELLE

I'll tell you how,
Thanks to their love, you've gained your freedom now.

JAILER

Wait for a safer moment. Our only thought
For now must be to run and not get caught.

ISABELLE

Let's hurry, then. But first you two must say
That you'll respect us till the wedding day.
If not, we won't—

CLINDOR

Lest that should trouble you,
I give my word.

JAILER

And, Lyse, you have mine, too.

ISABELLE

After that noble pledge, I have no fear.

JAILER

We're wasting time, friends. Let's get out of here.

Scene X

ALCANDRE

Fear not that they're in danger or disgrace!
Of their pursuers, none shall find their trace.

PRIDAMANT

I breathe at last.

ALCANDRE

After that happy date,
They rose in two years to a high estate.
I shall not tell you how their journey went,
Whether their seas were calm or turbulent
And by what art they prospered nonetheless;
'Twill do to tell you that they found success,
And, without weaving you a tedious story,
To show them to you in their present glory.
But since we pass now to a loftier plane,
I'll summon spirits of a finer grain.
Those who have brought to your astonished sight
Your son and Isabelle in love and flight
Would not be capable of showing you
The dazzling world which you are soon to view.

ACT V

Scene I

PRIDAMANT

How changed is Isabelle, how scintillating!

ALCANDRE

That's Lyse following her, as maid-in-waiting.
Now, once again, let nothing frighten you,
And do not leave this place until I do.
Do not forget my words, or you may die.

PRIDAMANT

In view of that, I promise to comply.

Scene II

ISABELLE (*as Hippolyte*); LYSE (*as Clarine*)

LYSE

What a long stroll we're taking! I beg your pardon,
But shall you spend the whole night in this garden?

ISABELLE

I can no longer hide why I am here;
A pain that's unconfessed grows more severe.
Prince Florilame—

LYSE

At present, he's away.

ISABELLE

That is the source of all my griefs today.
He's fond of us, his neighbors, and lets us use
That gate into his garden when we choose.
Princess Rosine and my unfaithful mate
Meet, when he's gone, by means of that same gate.
Tonight I plan to catch him, and make him see
That I'll not stand for infidelity.

LYSE

Madame, believe me, you'd do better if
You hid your feelings and didn't have a tiff.
Women gain nothing by a jealous scene;
It only makes the man more libertine;
For he's the master, and our plaints and prayers
Just make him obstinate in his affairs.

ISABELLE

Shall I ignore his treason? Not on your life!
She has his heart now, I but the name of wife!
Was it no crime to break his sacred pledge?
Should he not blush, then, for that sacrilege?

LYSE

That was the case once, but as things are now
A man is not constrained by pledge and vow:
For men, there is a different moral law;
What would disgrace us is for them no flaw;
Their honor feeds on what for us were shame;
It's having mistresses that gilds their fame.

ISABELLE

Pray say no more of these vain men to me,
Who base their honor on adultery.
If such a man became monogamous,
And therefore was accounted infamous,
I'd say his infamy was nobly gained,

And that it honored him to be disdained.
To be too faithful to one's wife, as some
Good husbands are, is sweet opprobrium.

LYSE

He's here, *Madame;* I heard the gate swing to.

ISABELLE

Let's hide.

LYSE

He sees you, and is following you.

Scene III

CLINDOR (*as Théagène*); ISABELLE (*as Hippolyte*);
LYSE (*as Clarine*)

CLINDOR

Why is it, Princess, that you're moved to flee?
Are these the joys of love you promised me?
Is this the way that lovers ought to meet?
Pray flee no more, and have no fears, my sweet:
The Prince is absent; my wife's asleep in bed.

ISABELLE

You're sure of that?

CLINDOR

O, gods; it's you instead!

ISABELLE

I'm wide awake, you traitor, and my sight
Is all too clear, though in the dark of night;
All my suspicions now are certainties,
And I've no doubt now of your treacheries.
By your own lips, your secret's been confessed!
Of all false lovers, you're the clumsiest;
Do you think that in these matters it's good sense

To take your wife into your confidence?
Where are your oaths to love no one but me?
What happened to your heart's integrity?
Recall, when you bestowed that heart, how great
A gap there was 'twixt you and my estate,
How many rivals I'd rejected who
Outshone a common soldier such as you,
How life in Father's house was sweet to share.
For you and poverty I left his care—
Yes, gladly was abducted, rather than
Be forced by him to wed another man.
I bore great hardships then; in every shape,
Danger and want attended our escape;
I suffered much till you were lifted by
Good luck to the noble rank you occupy.
If, to be happy, you now must be untrue,
Return me to the home I left for you.
I ventured all in loving you, not for fine
Rewards and glories, but that you might be mine.

CLINDOR

Don't blame me for your passion or your flight.
When love enslaves us, who can resist its might?
Love fused my image and your spirit's fire;
Not me you followed, but your own desire.
True, I was nothing then; but once you came
Away with me, our fortunes were the same;
Abducting you, I did not have in mind
The wealth which, after all, you left behind.

All we possessed, on my side, was a sword,
While love, on yours, was all you could afford:
The first has brought me fame in foreign climes;
I've risked death for the second, many times.
If now you miss your father, and are bored
With princesses and queens, with duke and lord,
Go home and see if with your father's gold
You can achieve such rank as here you hold.
Of what ills, after all, can you complain?
When have I domineered, or caused you pain?
Have I been cold to you, or shown you scorn?
Women! No stranger breed was ever born.
Let a husband's love for them so master him
That he obeys their least outrageous whim,
Heaps honors on them, does them kindly deeds,
Spares nothing to fulfill their slightest needs,
Yet if he breaks his marriage vow one bit
They act as if no crime could equal it;
It's perjury, murder, theft, and all things dire,
It's kill your father and set his house afire,
And so he suffers a volcanic fuss
Worse than what buried old Encèladus.

ISABELLE

I've said that when I ran away with you
I had no dreams of fame or power in view.
It was for you, you only, that I fled.
But since good fortune's gone now to your head,
Forget me. Think of how you've climbed so far:

'Twas Florilame who made you what you are.
You were a wandering soldier when his hand
Raised you from nothing to a high command,
And that first favor served in time to bring
You further favors from our lord the king.
With what great kindliness your friend the prince
Has worked for your advantage ever since,
Until, by this time, you are said to be,
Though less in rank, more powerful than he!
What brute would not be grateful? But instead
You thanklessly defile his marriage bed!
Excuse your brazen treachery, if you can;
Defend your falseness toward a generous man.
He's given you all; to rob him is your aim!
He made you a lord, and you besmirch his name!
O, ingrate! Can you have the hardihood
Thus to give evil in return for good?

CLINDOR

My soul (for that's the name I call you by,
And so shall call you till the day I die),
Think you that gratitude or mortal fear
Could govern me if you cannot, my dear?
Call me an ingrate, say I am forsworn,
But never think our sacred love outworn:
It is as potent now as at the start,
And if the passion that's waylaid my heart
Could have been stifled in its earliest hour,
The love I bear you would have had that power.

My honor chides me, but it speaks in vain;
You know that love's a force one can't restrain.
The god who made you leave your home for me,
And trade its comforts for my poverty—
That very god now makes me steal from you
The trifling matter of a sigh or two.
Permit me, then, this little escapade,
And have no fear that you shall be betrayed.
The love that is not built on virtue's rock
Soon passes, crumbling at the slightest shock,
But this our love is solid, and remains;
There honor brightly shines, and virtue reigns;
New charms enhance it as the years flow past,
And till we die its strong, sweet bonds shall last.
Once more, my soul, forgive this trick that's played
On me by Love, whose will must be obeyed;
Permit this foolish passion of a day,
Which shall not harm our love in any way.

ISABELLE

How fondly I delude myself! Although
Betrayed, I dream you love me even so;
I let sweet words enchant me; I gloss over
The crime because the criminal's my lover.
Forgive, dear husband, the intensity
Which this discovery provoked in me—
Though 'twould be unaffectionate and cold,
At such a moment, to be quite controlled.
Since now my youthful beauty's somewhat faded,

It's natural that your passion should be jaded,
And I believe you that this present flame
Will pass, and leave our married love the same.
But think now who it is that you pursue,
And what great danger she might be to you.
Be sly, be cautious, and dissimulate.
Love has no secrecy among the great;
The hangers-on who follow in their train
Are Argus-eyed; to them all things are plain,
And there is not a one of them who'd fail
To curry favor by a wicked tale.
Sooner or later, Florilame will find out,
By hunch or whisper, what you are about,
And then . . . I shudder at the very thought
Of what his rage will do when you are caught!
Since these diversions so appeal to you,
Pursue them, but be careful when you do.
I shall accept your trifling, if you'll swear
That you will trifle with the utmost care.

CLINDOR

Dear lady, must I say to you once more
That what I feel is well worth dying for?
My heart's too stricken, my reason too undone,
To fret about what dangers I may run.
My passion blinds me, and my head may be
The cost of this sweet prize, for all of me.
Time only can exhaust my passion's force;
It is a madness which must run its course.

ISABELLE

Fly to your death then, since it charms you so!
Be careless of your life as of my woe.
D'you think the outraged prince will be content
To settle for your death as punishment?
When, in a just revenge, he takes your life
For this base deed, who will protect your wife—
The widow of a foreign knave whose crime
He'll hasten to avenge a second time?
No, I'll not wait to see, when you are dead,
His further rage brought down upon my head,
Nor shall my honor, which is dear to me,
Be sacrificed to his malignity.
I shall forestall the shame I'm threatened by;
Since you don't care to live, I'll choose to die.
This body, which true love bade me confer
On you, will shortly fear no ravisher.
I've lived for love of you, but not the fate
Of serving your illustrious lady's mate.
Farewell, then: by my dying first, at least
The list of those you wrong will be decreased.

CLINDOR

Don't die, dear wife. No, rather look and see
The wondrous change your virtue's worked in me.
Despite my sins, you love me! You prefer
Death to the vile assaults you might incur!
I know not which I'm more admiring of—
Your boundless courage or your boundless love.

Both stagger me; again, I'm in your sway.
My base infatuation's now at bay;
It's done for; finished; and my ransomed soul
Has shaken off the chains of its control.
For a brief time, my balance was unsteady.
Let us forget it.

ISABELLE

It's forgot already.

CLINDOR

Let all the beauties of this world combine
Hereafter to besiege this heart of mine;
I shall resist the onslaught of their eyes,
And yours alone shall keep me pure and wise.

LYSE

Madame, there's someone coming.

Scene IV

CLINDOR (*as Théagène*); ISABELLE (*as Hippolyte*); LYSE
(*as Clarine*); ÉRASTE; TROOP OF FLORILAME'S SERVANTS

ÉRASTE (*Stabbing Clindor.*)

                    Knave, here's a greeting
From your mistress, who was sad to miss this meeting.

PRIDAMANT (*To Alcandre.*)

They're murdering him! Save him, o gods, I pray.

ÉRASTE

May all seducers perish in this way!

ISABELLE

What have you done, you butcher?

ÉRASTE

                      I've taught a great
Lesson for future times to contemplate—
The lesson that an ingrate who would stain
The honor of a prince is to be slain.
I've taken vengeance for Prince Florilame,
The outraged princess, and yourself, *Madame,*
And to you three have sacrificed the life

125

Of a cad who did not merit such a wife.
Accept the just chastisement of his nerve,
And don't regret the vengeance you deserve.
Farewell.

ISABELLE

You've only slaughtered half of him.
He lives in me as well. Come, let us swim
In blood, assassins! You must kill me, too.
Dear husband, in my arms they've murdered you,
And what my heart seemed darkly to foreknow
And darkly fear, could not avert the blow!
Alas, I now see clearly, and too late,
By these deep wounds, what was to be your fate.
If only . . . But I cannot breathe. This pain
Is more than breath or body can sustain.
It kills me, yet great joy's within my reach:
We'll be together . . .

LYSE

She's lost the power of speech.
My lady . . . She is dying, I'm afraid.
I'll hasten to the house and bring her aid.
(*Here a curtain is lowered, hiding the garden and
the bodies of Clindor and Isabelle, and the Magician
and Pridamant emerge from the cave.*)

Scene V

ALCANDRE

Thus Fortune mocks our hopes, and one and all
Upon its wheel are made to rise or fall,
And its caprice, which rules the universe,
Can soon turn any blessing to a curse.

PRIDAMANT

That thought's no comfort to a father, though
It might perhaps allay a trivial woe;
No, having seen the murder of my son,
My happiness destroyed, my hopes undone,
I'd be unnatural if I could be
Consoled by any such philosophy.
Alas! His poverty did not undo him;
Only good fortune could be fatal tò him.
I'll make no more lament than I have made:
A grieving sorrow hopes to be allayed,
But mine shall lead me dumbly where it must.
Farewell, I'll die now, since my son is dust.

ALCANDRE

A just despair, Sir, ought to be respected,
And what it urges should not be deflected.
Yes, follow your dear son without delay,
But promise not to take your life, I pray.
Allow your agonies of grief free rein,
And let this funeral scene increase your pain.
(*Now the curtain is raised again, and all the actors are
seen together with their manager. They count out money
on a table, each actor taking his share.*)

PRIDAMANT

Do the dead count money? What is happening there?

ALCANDRE

Each one, you'll note, is keen to get his share.

PRIDAMANT

I see Clindor, as he appeared in life!
His killers, too! And Lyse, and his wife!
What charm has solved their differences, and led
The living to assemble with the dead?

ALCANDRE

Thus does a troupe of actors from our stage
Divide the gate, and each receive his wage.
One slays, one dies, one causes tears to fall,
But it's the play alone that governs all.

Words make them fight; they die, if that's their part,
And, never taking any role to heart,
The traitor, the betrayed, the live, the slain,
Are, when the curtain falls, good friends again.
Your son and his companions stayed ahead
Of marshals and pursuers when they fled,
But when their lot grew needy and austere,
All four embraced the stage as a career.

PRIDAMANT

My son, an actor!

ALCANDRE

In that demanding art
They found a refuge and a world apart,
And all the things which you have seen of late—
Your son's adulterous love and bloody fate—
Were but the sad end of a tragic play
That's acted on the stage this very day
By him and others of his noble calling,
And which the whole of Paris finds enthralling.
They keep the proceeds, and the wardrobe which
I showed you earlier, so fine and rich,
Truly belongs to your Clindor, although
He wears it only when he's in a show.

PRIDAMANT

I thought his death was real; 'twas but an act;
And I feel very much disturbed, in fact.

Is this the high estate to which, in time,
His talent and good fortune were to climb?

ALCANDRE

Don't be disturbed, Sir. Nowadays, the stage
Is at so high a point, it's all the rage.
What in your youth was vulgar and debased
Is now the chief delight of men of taste,
The talk of Paris, the provincial's dream,
The pastime which our princes most esteem,
The people's joy, the pleasure of the great,
Who prize our drama at the highest rate,
While for those men of state by whose wise hands
Good order is maintained in many lands,
A charming spectacle can for an hour
Permit them to relax the reins of power.
Even our king, war's thunderbolt, whose name
Is feared throughout the universal frame,
Though crowned with laurels, deigns to give a glance
Quite often to the theatre of France.
It's there that you will find Parnassian wit;
Great minds devote their midnight oil to it;
And all Apollo's favorites give some part
Of their deep labors to that sovereign art.
Besides, if trades be judged by what they yield,
The theatre is a profitable field,
And in that pleasant enterprise your son
Earns far more than, at home, he could have done.

Dismiss all false impressions from your mind,
And don't lament a fate that's been so kind.

PRIDAMANT

I shall lament no longer. I hadn't known
How much his trade is better than my own.
I was upset at first, to tell the truth,
Remembering the theatre of my youth,
And thought ill of his choice, not knowing how
Uplifting and admired the stage is now.
But after what you've said, in great relief
I now retract my error and my grief.
Clindor has chosen wisely.

ALCANDRE

As you shall see.

PRIDAMANT

I shall. I'll leave tomorrow, I guarantee,
And fly toward Paris. Meanwhile, great Wizard, say
How I may thank you for your help today.

ALCANDRE

To serve good people is my chosen task:
To give you happiness is all I ask.
Farewell. Since you're content, I am the same.

PRIDAMANT

For such a gift, all thanks are trite and lame.
But, great Magician, what today you give
Shall ever be remembered while I live.

CURTAIN